T0355990

# Learn Korean Vocabulary Using Double Memory Mnemonics

Brian Brown

Order this book online at www.trafford.com
or email orders@trafford.com

Most Trafford titles are also available at major online book retailers.

Print information available on the last page.

ISBN: 978-1-6987-1851-4 (sc)
ISBN: 978-1-6987-1852-1 (e)
Library of Congress Control Number: 2025902436

*Trafford rev. 02/06/2025*

 www.trafford.com
**North America & international**
toll-free: 844-688-6899 (USA & Canada)
fax: 812 355 4082

# INTRODUCTION

Here are some conventions in this book:

(1) I use the Revised Romanization System for Korean (but not Hangcul)

(2) These are simply suggestions, and may not always work for everyone.

(3) The pronunciations may not always be totally accurate; the idea is to prompt or trigger associations.

A parapharased quote from the book "Teach Yourself Korean" (Vincent and Yeon):

"The first thing to remember is this: don't be discouraged by how different or difficult it appears at first. It is different, and it is difficult. But, as long as you keep going, you will soon recognize the patterns and understand and how Korean sentences and vocabulary work."

I wish you luck and success in your Korean language studies

1.  ladder: **sa-da-ri** (n.)
    Sad Ari fell off the ladder, and injured himself.

2.  wait: **gi-da-ri-da** (v.)
    The ghee, Dari, will have to wait. The butter is not clarified yet. Just wait!

3.  vulgar (rude language): **jeo-sok-an** (adj.)
    I ("jeo", similar to French "je") soak Anne in a barrel, for using vulgar language. (v. = jeo-sok-ha-da, to be vulgar)

4.  voyage: **yeo-haeng** (n.)
    If yuh hang around here for too long, you'll get wanderlust, and want to voyage. (v. = yeo-haeng-ha-da; to voyage, travel)

5.  to joke around: **nong-dam-ha-da** (v.)
    Non! (as in French, "NOHNG!") Damn! Hada, don't joke around! It's no laughing matter! (n. = nong-dam)

6.  tattoo: **mun-sin** (n.)
    Imagine that Mr. Sheen has a tattoo of the moon.

7.  tax money: **Se-geum** (n.)
    Say, Kermit, how much tax money do you have to pay each year?

1

8. teach: **ga-reu-chi-da** (v.)
Imagine that you <u>teach</u> as a visiting prof in <u>Karachi</u>, Pakistan.

9. temple: **sa-won** (n.)
<u>Lisa won</u> a guided tour to visit the ancient <u>temples</u>.

10. orchard: **gwa-su-won** (n.)
- <u>Sue won</u> tickets to see the rock band <u>GWAR</u>!
- That's great, because she makes little money working in an <u>orchard</u>.

11. Science: **gwa-hak** (n.)
(gwa = GWAR; hak = stork bird or crane bird)
- You're a bad student! Instead of studying <u>cranes and storks</u> (hak) in <u>Science</u> class, you're listening to <u>GWAR</u>! (gwa)

12. understand: **i-hae-ha-da** (v.)
(i = tooth, so MAD magazine's mascot, Alfred E. Neuman; hae = sea or ocean)
<u>Alfred E. Neuman</u> (i) <u>understands</u> that it's not good to fool around while at <u>sea</u> (hae).

13. to be ordinary: **pyeong-beom-ha-da** (v.)
Imagine that it's better to be <u>ordinary</u>, than to be a do<u>pey young bum</u> who just smokes weed and never works.
(adj. = pyeong-beom-han)

14. emphasize: **gang-jo-ha-da**
The pro-wrestler King <u>Kong</u> (gang) Bundy will fight the Nintendo boxer Glass Joe (jo) in a match. I <u>emphasize</u>, Joe will not last long!

15. fool (n): **ba-bo** (n.)
- <u>Pa, bo</u> keeps prattling like a damn <u>fool</u>.
- He'd better stop, before I lose my cool.

16. basket: **ba-gu-ni** (n.)
- <u>Pa, goony</u> thugs have stolen our <u>basket</u>!
- If I catch them, they'll end up in a casket!

17. debris: **pa-pyeon** (n.)
Imagine a ceramic <u>butterfly</u> (in French, <u>papillon</u>, or PA-PEE-YOHNG) that falls down, and breaks into <u>debris</u> (broken fragments).

18. to have a meal, to dine: **sik-sa-ha-da** (v)
<u>Shiksas</u> (non-Jewish women and girls) may not usually like <u>to have</u> Jewish <u>meals</u>, but sometimes they do.
(n. = "sik-sa", meal).

19. mosquito: **mo-gi** (n)
Imagine that Japanese scientist Ken <u>Mogi</u> has invented a new <u>mosquito</u> repellent.

20. moss (plant): **ikki** (n.)
That <u>moss</u> is really "<u>icky</u>" for some reason.

21. moth: **na-bang**
- <u>Nah, bong</u>s don't attract <u>moth</u>s.
It takes light to do that.

22. butterfly (insect): **na-bi** (n.)
<u>Nah, Bee</u>, <u>butterflies</u> are not the same as moths, though they're related.

23. rescue: **gu-jo-ha-da** (v.)
Imagine you <u>rescue</u> someone from <u>Cujo</u>, the vicious dog from the Stephen King novel.

24. resign: **sa-jik-a-da** (v.)
Imagine that Li<u>sa squeak</u>ed (squeak: jik) when Beth Harmon played a brilliant chess move, then <u>resign</u>ed. (re: "The Queen's Gambit.") (resignation = sa-jik)

25. restaurant: **sik-dang**
Imagine: the <u>Sheik</u> (sik) had a great Persian <u>soup</u> (dang, close to "tang") in his <u>restaurant</u>.

26. problem: **mun-je**
- If you <u>moon Jay</u>, you'll have a <u>problem</u>. He'll kick the crap outta ya.

27. key: **yeol-soe**
- <u>You'll sway</u> with ectasy, when they award you the <u>key</u> to the city.

28. to do: **ha-da** (v.)
Whatever <u>Hada</u> wants <u>to do</u>, is what she does.

29. compare: **bi-gyo-ha-da** (v.)
When K-pop singer <u>Rain</u> (bi) performed at a concert in To<u>kyo</u> (gyo), many fans <u>compared</u> him to Michael Jackson.

30. prepare: **jun-bi-ha-da** (v.)
Imagine that you <u>prepare</u> a <u>June</u> Bug cocktail, while listening to K-pop singer <u>Rain</u> (bi).

31. quilt: **nu-bi-i-bul**
Imagine a <u>quilt</u> with an image of <u>Scooby-Doo</u> on it.

32. sigh: **han-sum-swi-da** (v.)
A woman sees a <u>handsome</u> guy, and <u>sighs</u>. (n. = han-sum)

33. trivial, minor: **sa-so-ha-da**
Will <u>Sasso</u> is no <u>minor</u> actor; he has starred in many movies and T.V. shows.

34. person, people: **sa-ram**
Li<u>sa, ram</u> home the point that the poor and homeless are <u>people</u>, just like everyone else.

35. to jump to conclusions: **pi-yak-ha-da** (v.)
Regarding K-pop star <u>Rain</u> (Bi): <u>yak</u>kers <u>jump to conclusions</u> and gossip about him. I just take it with a grain of salt.

36. to obey: **bok-jong-ha-da** (v.)
(Let "bok" be "pig", like "pig in a <u>poke</u>." Also "bok" can be good luck, and pigs are lucky in some cultures. Let "jong" be "bell.")
If you ring the <u>bell</u>. (jong), <u>Hada</u>, the <u>pigs</u> will <u>obey</u> you.

37. to approve, permit: **seung-nak-ha-da** (v.)
("seung" means "victory" or "winning.")
If you <u>win</u> (seung) even a <u>neck</u>-and-<u>neck</u> (nak) <u>victory</u>, you'll have <u>approval</u> (seung-nak) to implement your policies.

38. diarrhea: **seol-sa** (n.)
Imagine you eat really bad <u>salsa</u> sauce, and then get <u>diarrhea</u> (seol-sa).

39. dictator: **dok-jae-ja** (n.)
If you <u>toke, Jay,</u> while driving your <u>car</u> ("ja" → "cha" or car), then the dictator will kill you, even if you don't crash.

40. weasel (animal): **jok-je-bi** (n.)
Don't <u>joke, Jay! Be</u> serious! It's not funny, that Kopi Luwak <u>weasels</u> poop out the coffee beans, which folks drink later!

41. dice (cubes): **ju-sa-wi** (n.)
Mr. <u>Chu saw wee</u> <u>dice</u> that were strange, because they always rolled high numbers.

42. dictionary: **sa-jeon** (n.)
Li<u>sa, "jeon"</u> (Korean pancakes) should be readily found in the culinary <u>dictionary</u>,

43. apple (fruit): **sa-gwa** (n.)
Li<u>sa, GWA</u>R (the rock group) is not on Apple Records®, I don't think,

44. love: **sa-rang** (n.)
Li<u>sa, wrong</u>ly - directed <u>love</u> is not a good thing. (v. = sa-rang-ha-da)

45. gift, present: **seon-mul** (n.)
<u>Son</u>, <u>water</u> (<u>mul</u>) such as Evian®, might be a <u>good gift</u> for someone who drinks a lot of it.

46. install: **seol-chi-ha-da** (v.)
The "<u>sull</u>" (sullen) <u>Chi</u>huahua cheered up after we <u>instal</u>led a small treadmill for him (seol-chi = installation)

47. Survive: **saeng-jon-ha-da** (v.)
Sang Joan: "I will survive, no matter how much crap people throw at me!"
(survival = saeng-jon; survivor = saeng-jon-ja)

48. sightseeing: **gwan-gwang** (n.)
(gwan = Billy Kwan, the Kung fu character from the U.S. comedy show "Almost Live!"; gwang = Gwangju City, S. Korea).
Imagine that Billy Kwan (gwan) goes on a sightseeing tour of Gwangju.)

49. to be similar: **yu-sa-ha-da**
Imagine that you saw Hada walking with someone who looked similar (it was her sister.)

50. to be similar: bi-seut-an (adj.); **bi-seut-ha-da** (v.)
Imagine that Bee's (bi) shirt (seut) is similar to Hada's (ha-da)

51. just, only: **dan**
Imagine that Marvel supervillain Fancy Dan is only 5 feet tall, but he's a formidable fighter.

52. romantic: **nang-man-jeok-in** (adj.)
Don't be a nong (nang), man! Chuck insisted. You need to act romantic, if you hope to impress her!

53. rose (flower): **jang-mi**
Imagine that Mr. Chong (jang) says, "Ah, me! I should have brought a rose!"

54. restore: **bok-won-ha-da**
(Let "bok" be "pig", e.g. "pig in a poke.")
The pig (bok) won a top prize, which restored his "not-for-slaughter" status.

55. slaughter, massacre (people): **hak-sal-ha-da** (v.)
If you hock Sal's CD's and books without telling him and getting his "OK," he'll slaughter ya.

56. slaughter (animals): **do-chuk-ha-da** (v.)
Doh! This porridge (chuk → juk) is awful! It's only fit for animals to be slaughtered.

57. snail: **dal-paeng-i** (n.)
Imagine that tall penguins are only slightly faster than snails.

58. fake, counterfeit: **wi-jo-jok-in** (adj.)
(Let "jo" be Nintendo boxer "Glass Joe")
Imagine that "wee Joe" chucks fake punches often, but seldom lands real ones. (wi-jo-ha-da = to forge, make a fake or forgery)

59. to be good, or good-natured: **cha-ka-da**
Imagine that in most card games, a Jack is a good card to have.

60. hibernate: **dong-myeon-ha-da** (v.)
(Let "dong" be Japan, as it means "the East."
Let "myeon" mean "thin noodles".)
Imagine that, before <u>Japan</u>ese bears
<u>hibernate</u>, they eat a lot of "<u>myeon</u>."
(n. = "dong-myeon," hibernation)

61. to be lonely or isolated: **go-dok-ha-da** (v.)
(Let "go" be "nose"; "go" → "ko") (Let
"dok" be Germany; dok-il)
Imagine that, if you have a big <u>nose</u> (go →
ko) in <u>Germany</u> (dok-il), then you won't <u>be
lonely</u>; many people there have a big schnozz.

62. to improve: **gae-seon-ha-da** (v.)
Your <u>dog</u> (= gae), <u>son</u>, needs to <u>improve</u>. You
need to walk him more, and feed him better
food.

63. symbol: **sang-jing** (n.)
For a <u>song jing</u>le, some written musical notes
are a <u>symbol</u>.

64. myth: **sin-hwa** (n.)
Mr. <u>Sheen, hwa</u>! has many <u>myths</u> associated
with him.

65. awful, terrible: **kkeum-jjik-an** (adj.)
You <u>Kerm! Cheek</u> and awful language will
never serve you well!

66. to err, make a mistake: **sil-su-ha-da** (v.)
Don't make a <u>mistake</u> and slander or libel that politician, 'cause <u>she'll sue</u> you into oblivian!
(n. = sil-su; "mistake"; "error")

67. complicated, complex: **bok-jap-an** (adj.)
The international trade regime is <u>complicated</u>, so Japan's trade partners shouldn't <u>poke Japan</u> with strong measures.

68. to be concerned, worried: **geok-jeong-ha-da** (v.)
Imagine that your "metalhead" friends will think you're a bit of a "<u>cuck</u>" (geok) if they find out you listen to the pop band Wang Chung, so you're a bit <u>concerned</u>.

69. to persist, continue: **gye-sok-ha-da**
<u>Kay, soak Hada</u> in the sink/<u>continue</u> till she stops acting like a fink!
(Note: this one is similar to the "empapar" jingle in "The Intermediate Spanish Memory Book" by Harrison and Welker. Please buy it if you're studying Spanish!)

70. devil: **akma** (pron. = akma → angma) (n.)
Imagine Bobby Boucher (Adam Sandler) from the comedy (The Waterboy"):

"Ach, mama! Not everyone and everything is the Devil!"

71.  to die, perish: **sa-mang-ha-da** (v.)
     (Let "sa" be number 4 → Marvel superheroes "The Fantastic Four. Let "mang" be Marvel supervillain "Mongu.")

     Imagine that, if Mongu (mang) were to fight the Fantastic Four, he would die, though he could take them individually.

72.  garbage, trash, rubbish: **sseu-re-gi**
     - Sir Ray, ghee is O.K. in Indian food, in small amounts.
     - Yes, but too much can make a dish fit for the garbage can.

73.  to spend (time, money, effort): **so-bi-ha-da** (v.)
     - So, Bee had a shopping spree today?
     - Yep. She practically spent all her money away!

74.  side dish(es): **ban-chan**
     We ban Chan from our dinner table, because he eats all our side dishes!

75.  to nag or nit pick: **jan-so-ri-ha-da** (v)
     Chan (jan), sorry (so-ri) for nagging you so much/But, you do need to take shorter breaks at lunch!

76. magnet: **ja-seok** (n.)
- This lemony <u>car</u> (ja → cha) really <u>sucks</u>, it's a hunk of shirt.
- Then give it to the junk yard, to have it raised by a big <u>magnet</u>!

77. descendant: **ja-son** (n.)
Imagine that <u>Jason</u> (from Friday the 13<sup>th</sup>) was <u>descended</u> (or a <u>descendant</u>) from other murderous psychos.

78. effective: **hyo-gwa-jeok-in** (adj.)
Hyo! <u>GWAR</u>, <u>Chuck</u>, has stage outfits that are very <u>effective</u>, though perhaps not quite as effective as those of kiss.

79. to edit, arrange: **pyeon-jip-ha-da**
(Let "pyeon" be "peon" or "pawn"; let "jip" be "house.") Imagine that you have to <u>edit</u> a chess magazine called "<u>House</u> (jip) of <u>Pawns</u>. (pyeon.)"

80. to correct, edit: **gyo-jeong-ha-da**
Imagine that in To<u>kyo</u> (gyo), (Wang) <u>Chung</u> (UK pop group; "jeong") <u>corrected</u> some spoken mistakes they'd been making in Japanese language.

81. education, teaching: **gyo-yuk**
In To<u>kyo</u> (gyo), <u>six</u> (= yuk) universities provide <u>education</u> in rare languages.

82. to be easy, not difficult: **su-wol-ha-da** (v.)
<u>Sue, wool</u> sweaters are <u>not hard</u> to knit/you need to sit down, and put your mind to it.

83. jewel, gem: **bo-seok**
<u>Bo, suck</u> up the bill, and pay for the <u>jewel</u>/If you thought it would be cheap, then you're a darn fool.

84. join, connect: **yeon-gyeol-ha-da**
(Let "yeon" be "kite." Let "gyeol" be "keel"). Imagine that, while flying a <u>kite</u> (yeon), you get stomach cramps, and <u>keel</u> (gyeol) over, and lose the <u>connect</u>ion with the string and kite. (n. = yeon-gyeol, "connection", "tie", "link")

85. dumpling: **man-du**
"Some of the best <u>dumplings</u> in Asia are found in Khat<u>mandu</u>, Nepal."

86. protect: **bo-ho-ha-da**
<u>Bo, ho! Had a</u> desire to <u>protect</u>/The subway commuters, from crooks picking their pockets.

87. strict, stern: **eom-gyeok-han** (adj)
Um, G.I.U.K. (Greenland, Iceland, U.K.) territories had a strict policy against overfishing in their waters.
(v. = eom-gyeok-ha-da; "to be strict")

88. shocking: **chung-gyeok-jeok-in** (adj.)
(Let "chung" be "China", as it's close to "jung-guk.")
Imagine that Chuck (jeok) found it shocking to learn that China (jung) had surpassed the G.I.U.K. (gyeok) territories in almost every measure.

89. popular: **in-gi-in-neun**
In this Italian restaurant, the squid pasta is the most popular dish, though it's quite inky.

90. to be well-behaved: **yam-jeom-ha-da** (v.)
- Oh, awesome! Baked yams! (yam)
- Chum (jeom), you'll only get one if you're well-behaved.

91. to forbid, ban, prohibit: **geum-ji-ha-da** (v.)
Imagine that the wealthy actress had a gold (geum) collar-wearing Chihuahua (ji), which she forbade going outside without her.

92. excellent, superb, etc.: **hul-lyung-han** (adj.)
For some grunge fans Mötley Crüe's song "Hooligan's Holiday" was an excellent tune. (this is a rough approximation)

93. excellent, outstanding: **u-su-han** (adj.)
You watch a basketball match, and think, "Ooh! Sue handles the ball in an outstanding way!"

94. graceful, elegant or dashing: **u-a-han**
Imagine that a young Han Solo (from "Star Wars" films) was very dashing. Many women would think, "Ooh! Ah! Han is so dashing!

95. to reform (v.): **gae-hyeok-ha-da** (v.)
Imagine someone saying, "The dog (= gae) meat industry, hyuck! (= hyeok) had a need to reform! (n = gae-hyeok, "reformation")

96. to flatter: **a-bu-ha-da**
In Abu Dhabi, he sometimes flattered his boss.

97. hut, cabin, lodge, hovel: **o-du-mak-jip**
- Oh, do Mack jeep dealerships exist in this area?
- Yes, there's one across from the "Pizza Hut."®

98. to reconcile, make up with: **hwa-hae-ha-da**
(Let "hwa" be "flower." Let "hae" be "sea.")
Imagine: you're with your estranged spouse by the <u>sea</u> (hae), and you proffer <u>flowers</u> (hwa), and try to <u>reconcile</u>.

99. to conquer or overcome: **geuk-bok-ha-da**
(Let "geuk" be Captain <u>Kirk</u> from Star Trek. Let "bok" be "pig", from "pig in a <u>poke</u>.)
Captain James <u>Kirk</u> (geuk) <u>conquered</u> a planet, and had to <u>overcome</u> a race of <u>pig</u>-like aliens there.

100. annoying, irritating: **seong-ga-shin**
(Let "seong" be "castle." Let "ga" be a "crow" or raven, from "Caw!" sound. Let "shin" be a <u>god</u>-like character.)
Imagine playing a computer game, in which you have to free people from a <u>castle</u> (seong), while avoiding <u>crows</u> and a <u>god</u> like enemy. You think, "This game is <u>annoy</u>ingly difficult to beat!"

101. to conquer: **jeong-bok-ha-da**
You're saving up money for a Wang <u>Chung</u> concert. You have to <u>conquer</u> your desire to open your <u>piggy</u> bank (bok, see elsewhere for explanation) for other stuff.

102. to defeat (or to win): **i-gi-da** (v.)
Imagine that you <u>defeat</u> several other contestants in a "rock trivia" game, and you <u>win</u> albums by <u>Iggy</u> Pop.

103. to be defeated, beaten: **pae-bae-ha-da**
Imagine that someone decides to <u>pay bay</u> - dwellers to keep up the area, so they're not <u>defeated</u> by sundry social problems.

104. witness, observe: **mok-gyeok-ha-da** (v.)
(Let "mok" be a <u>moke</u>, or low-quality horse. Let "gyeok" be category or class of something.)
- I <u>observe</u> that these <u>mokes</u> (<u>mok</u>) belong to the same <u>category</u> (gyeok).

105. to insult: **mo-yok-ha-da** (v.)
Imagine <u>Moe</u> (from the Simpsons cartoon) responding to an insult by throwing egg <u>yolk</u> (yok) at someone.

106. republic: **gong-hwa-guk** (n.)
(Let "gong" be "<u>bean</u>" (gong → kong).)
- Coffee <u>beans (gong), hwa! Kooky</u> as it may sound, are the basis of this <u>republic</u>!

107. to think, to deem: **saeng-gak-ha-da**
When she <u>sang, gawk</u>ers <u>thought</u> she was the worst singer ever.

108. level, standard: **su-jun** (n.)
Sue, June Bug cocktails at this bar, are not up to standard.

109. essay: **su-pil** (n.)
Sue, peel the potatoes yourself. I have to work on my essay; it's due tomorrow!

110. check, cheque (U.K.): **su-pyo** (n.)
Sue, P.O. boxes are not a good place to store cheques!

111. sharp: **ppyo-jok-an** (adj)
- It's not a good idea to make a "B.O. joke", Han. Here, there are people with sharp weapons.

112. sneaky, tricky, sly: **gyo-hwal-han**
Imagine that, in Tokyo, behind a wall (close to "hwal"), Han used tricky shots from his ray gun to beat Godzilla.

113. truth: **sa-sil** or **jin-sil**
- Lisa, she'll always tell the truth. Jean, she'll usually tell the truth, but not always. (sincere, truthful = jin-sil-han)

114. lie (untruth): **geo-jin-mal** (n.)
- Guh! Gene, mal ware always tells a lie! Please don't click on it.

115. shelf: **seon-ban** (n.)
- <u>Son, ban</u> people from our shop, if they have put bubble-gum on our shelves!

116. to transport: **un-ban-ha-da** (v.)
(Let "un" be "one", as in Catalan language. Let "ban" be "half.")
- <u>One</u> (un) <u>half</u> (ban) of the class was transported to the zoo; the other half stayed at the school.

117. to translate or interpret (spoken words): **tong-yeok-ha-da** (v.)
(Let "tong" be "can".)
- The drink in that <u>can</u> (tong), <u>yuck</u>! <u>had a</u> terrible taste! How can I <u>translate</u> that into the local language?

118. to chat: **jap-dam-ha-da**
- That <u>chap, damn</u>! spends also his time chatting! (n = jap-dam, a chat)

119. to profane or defile: **mo-dok-ha-da**
Imagine that many Marvel fans found the movie version of supervillain <u>Modok</u> (in the Ant-Man and the Wasp film) to be a <u>profanation or blasphemy</u> of the comic book original (n. = mo-dok)

120. to be rude: **mu-rye-ha-da**
Imagine that <u>Murray</u> <u>had a</u> knack for writing <u>rude</u>, yet comic and intriguing lyrics, for the Dayglos (a punk rock band.) (adj. = mu-rye-han)

121. runway (airport): **hwal-ju-ro** (n.)
From the airport <u>wall</u> (close to "hwal"), I could hear the "<u>Choo</u>!" (ju) of a nearby train, and see the <u>low</u> (row) plane landing on the <u>runway.</u>

122. Stethoscope: **cheong-jin-gi** (n.)
- Where's the <u>stethoscope</u>?
- It's in the locker that has stickers of Wang <u>Chung</u> (UK pop band), <u>Gene</u> Simmons (rock star), and <u>Superman</u> (ki; giant <u>key</u> from Fortress of Solitude.)

123. to faint, pass out: **gi-jeol-ha-da**
(Let "gi" be <u>Superman</u>; see #120. Let "jeol" be <u>Iron Man</u> (jeol → cheol, or "steel" which is similar.)
Imagine: <u>Superman</u> fights <u>Iron Man</u>; the latter uses a kryptonite repulsor ray, causing Superman to <u>faint</u>.

124. beer: **maek-ju**
At a McDonald's in Europe, Mr. <u>Chu</u> (ju) had a Big <u>Mac</u>® burger and a <u>beer</u>.

125. to bet, gamble: **nae-gi-ha-da** (v.)
- <u>Naggy Hada</u> would scold her friends not to <u>bet</u> or <u>gamble</u>.

126. to gamble: **do-bak-ha-da**
- To get her <u>dough back, Hada</u> kept <u>gambling</u> (and losing).

127. spoil, mess up: **mang-chi-da**
- If you add <u>mango</u> to <u>chee</u>se, it'll <u>mess it up</u>!

128. to train, coach, teach: **hul-lyeon-ha-da** (v.)
He's the <u>coach</u> with <u>who Leon</u> will train. (n. = hul-lyeon, "training" or "coaching.")

129. alarm clock: **ja-myeong-jong**
You want to get up early for <u>tea</u> (ja → cha). So, you set your <u>alarm clock</u>. It says your <u>name</u> (<u>myeong</u>), and has a <u>bell</u> (jong) to wake you.

130. start, begin, commence: **si-jak-ha-da**
At a casino, you see a player who looks a bit like <u>Xi</u> Jinping (<u>si</u>). He gets two <u>Jacks</u> (<u>jak</u>) and wins the first Blackjack round. He says, "Good <u>start</u>!" (n. = si-jak)

131. to be shabby, decrepit: **cho-ra-ha-da**
Imagine: the Nintendo® boxer Glass <u>Joe</u> (jo → cho) is so <u>decrepit</u>, any <u>raw</u> boxer can beat him.

132. to collect, gather: **su-jip-ha-da**
- <u>Sue, cheap</u> as she is, only <u>collects</u> low-value stamps, coins and sports cards. (n. = su-jip, "collection")

133. hard, difficult: **eo-ryeo-wo-yo** (polite present tense)
- It's <u>hard</u> to stay in shape, if <u>Oreo</u>® (eo-ryeo) cookies is all you eat! (adj. = eo-ryeo-un)

134. string, cord, shoelace: **kkeun**
Imagine: <u>Colone</u>l (<u>kkeun</u>) Sanders always tied his <u>shoelaces</u> (<u>kkeun</u>) properly, and looked dapper.

135. ginseng: **in-sam** (n.)
- <u>E'en Sam</u>, who dislikes Oriental medicine, finds <u>ginseng</u> tasty and useful.

136. frivolous: **gyeong-bak-han**
- Those dor<u>ky young backhan</u>ded guys called my work <u>frivolous</u>, though they'd praised it before.

137. to be excessive or extreme: **gwa-do-ha-da**
- The rock band <u>GWAR</u> (gwa), <u>though</u> (do) garbed in outrageous outfits, are not known for <u>excessive</u> antics off-stage.

138. to be famous: **yu-myeong-han**
(Let "yu" be Uncle Sam, e.g. "I Want You.")

- Uncle Sam's (yu) name (myeong) and image are famous throughout the world.

139. eyepatch: **an-dae**
- Anne lost an eye when she was caught up in a rioting crowd (dae → tte), so now she wears an eyepatch.

140. teahouse: **da-bang** (n.)
Imagine going to a teahouse (da-bang), in the city of Dabang, Philippines.

141. apricot: **sal-gu** (n.)
- Sal, goo from apricot pulp will not make a good treat, I don't think.

142. narrow-minded: **pyeon-hyeop-an**
- Despite Bobby Fischer's genius with pawns (pyeon), knights (horses; "giddy up; hyeop) and other chess pieces, he could be very narrow-minded.

143. environment, surroundings: **hwan-gyeong**
- Juan (close to "hwan"), "dorky" young people need an environment that's conducive to more intellectual hobbies.

144. to promise: **yak-sok-ha-da** (v.)
- Before we yak, soak Hada in tar and feather her/Because she keeps her promises, never!

145. choreography: **an-mu** (n.)

- In a video, <u>An</u>ne (<u>an</u>) is milking some <u>cows</u> (<u>moo</u> → <u>mu</u>), and then does a <u>choreographed</u> song and dance.

146. camouflage, disguise: **wi-jang-ha-da**

- Imagine saying, <u>Oui</u> (wi), <u>Jean</u> (jang; French male name "Jean" → "ZHAHNG", close to "jang."), in the army, you have to learn how to do <u>camouflage</u>. (n. = wi-jang)

147. monster: **goe-mul**

Imagine: at a <u>quay</u> (<u>goe</u>, "dock"), a Loch Ness <u>Monster</u> comes out of the <u>water</u> (<u>mul</u>).

148. abandon, or give up: **po-gi-ha-da** (v.)

- That officer is clearly "<u>pogue-y</u>", so he should <u>give up</u> trying to act tough.

149. big, large: **keun** (adj.)

- <u>Colone</u>l Sanders made <u>big</u> (<u>keun</u>) money from KFC®.

150. to misunderstand: **o-hae-ha-da** (v.)

(Let "o" be the number "five". Let "hae" be "sea".)

- The fishermen <u>misunderstood</u>, that they weren't allowed to fish near the <u>five</u> (<u>o</u>) islands in this part of the <u>sea</u> (hae).

151. delay, postpone: **ji-yeon-ha-da** (v.)
- Do you want to fly <u>kites</u> (<u>yeon</u>) with us, <u>Hada</u>?
- I have to take my <u>Chi</u>huahua (ji) to the vet, so I need to <u>postpone</u>. (n. = ji-yeon; a "delay" or "postponement.")

152. potato: **gam-ja** (n.)
- If some people smoke <u>ganja</u> (close to gam-ja), then they might have the "munchies" for a baked <u>potato</u> (gam-ja).

153. slope, incline (n.): **gyeong-sa-myeon**
- A group of gee<u>ky young</u> guys (<u>gyeong</u>) (or dor<u>ky young</u> guys) <u>saw</u> (<u>sa</u>) a <u>myeon</u> (noodle) restaurant at the top of a <u>slope</u>, and decided to eat there.

154. headquarters: **bon-bu** (n.)
- The headquarters is located next to that <u>phone boo</u>th. (bon-bu)

155. crane (for building): **gi-jung-gi** (n.)
(Let "gi" be Superman; see earlier explanation. Let "jung" be a <u>China</u>town, from "jung-guk.")
Imagine that Lex Luthor causes a pair of <u>cranes</u> to fall in <u>China</u>town, but Superman prevents them from crashing down.

156. mop (for cleaning): **dae-geol-le** (n.)
(Let "dae" be like the word for <u>tea</u> in Spanish or French, sounds like "TAY." The last two syllables remind me of "goalie.")
Imagine: after having <u>tea</u> (dae), you have a "lawn soccer" match, and you're one of the <u>goalies</u>.

157. envelope, small bag: **bong-tu**
You're on a <u>Boeing</u> (like "bong" said fast) flight, and you get badly airsick, so you need <u>two</u> (<u>tu</u>) airsickness bags.

158. to try, attempt: **si-do-ha-da**
- <u>See, dough</u> isn't really that hard to earn/But you have to work hard, and <u>try</u> to learn.

159. free, no charge: **mu-ryo** (ha-da)
- Ra<u>mu</u>, <u>Rio</u> is not the most expensive city one can see/But, don't expect to get things for <u>free</u>!

160. lava: **yong-am** (n.)
- A <u>dragon</u> (<u>yong</u>) has <u>cancer</u> (<u>am</u>), and it's in much pain. It breathes a lot of fire, and causes a <u>lava</u> landslide.

161. cutting board: **do-ma** (n.)
- Where should I put the <u>dough, Ma</u>?
- On the <u>cutting board</u>, of course!

162. palace: **gung-jeon** (n.)
Around the <u>palace</u>, pigeons are <u>cooing</u> ("gung" said fast). The royals are inside, making <u>jeon</u> (Korean pancakes).

163. soap: **bi-nu**
Imagine owning a pet <u>gnu</u> (nu, "wildebeest"). When it <u>rains</u> (bi), you bathe it with <u>soap</u>.

164. to be interested in: **gwan-sim-ha-da**
(Let "gwan" be Billy Kwan, a Bruce Lee-type character from the T.V. comedy "Almost Live!")
- Billy <u>Kwan seem</u>s (gwan-sim) to <u>be interested in</u> mixed martial arts, and not just Kung Fu.

165. monkey: **won-sung-i**
- If you're a legal <u>one suing</u> ("sung" said fast) <u>e</u>vil (<u>i</u>) blokes/You should be well-versed, and not a <u>monkey</u> who's a joke!

166. to persist: **go-jip-ha-da**
- <u>Coe, cheap Hada</u> <u>persists</u> in buying, well, dirt-cheap items, though the quality is awful.

167. to film (a story): **chwal-yeong-ha-da**
Imagine: hard rock band <u>AC/DC</u> (Malcom <u>Young</u> and <u>Angus Young</u> were members; <u>yeong</u>) had a concert in Montreal, Canada.

A couple of cameramen were speaking joual (chwal) (a Quebec French dialect), and filming the concert.

168. bucket, pail: **yang-dong-i**

(Let "yang" be "Shaun the Sheep®". Let "dong" be Homer Simpson, ie. "doh-ing" said fast. Let "i" be Alfred E. Neuman, the MAD mascot missing one tooth.)

Imagine an animation studio, and these 3 characters are using buckets and mops to clean the floors.

169. to persist: **ji-sok-ha-da**

- Suji, soak Hada in soapy water, to assuage my wrath/Because she persists, in not taking a bath!

170. road: **do-ro**

- In Pamplona, Spain, people run down the road (do-ro) with "toros" (bulls) chasing them!

171. fantastic, cool, splendid, awesome, etc.: **gwaeng-jang-han**

Imagine: Han is resting and fishing at a quay ("quay-ing" said quickly) and eating bulgogi with jang (pepper paste). He catches a big fish, and shouts, "Fantastic!"

172. to subscribe: **gu-dok-ha-da**
- I'm so into studying <u>German</u> (<u>dok</u>-il-eo), that I <u>subscribe</u> to <u>nine</u> (<u>gu</u>) German newspapers and magazines!

173. to stimulate: **ja-geuk-ha-da**
- When <u>Kirk</u> (geuk) drinks <u>tea</u> (<u>ja</u> → <u>cha</u>), it's <u>stimulating</u>.

174. debt: **bit** (n.)
- If you don't pay your <u>debt</u> (<u>bit</u>), thugs may <u>beat</u> you up.

175. debt: **bu-chae** (n.)
Imagine: Bobby <u>Boucher</u> (close to <u>bu-chae</u>) (from The Waterboy) had much <u>debt</u>.

176. luxury: **sa-chi**
- Imagine that the famous Akita dog <u>Hachi</u> (rhymes with <u>sa-chi</u>) lived in <u>luxury</u> (sa-chi).

177. cram school: **ha-gwon**
- That <u>hog won</u> enough lotto money, to buy up all the <u>cram schools</u> (ha-gwon)!

178. to plan: **gye-hoek-ha-da** (v.)
- <u>Kay, wake Hada</u> up, so we can <u>plan</u> our next move! (rough device)

179. plum (fruit): **ja-du**

- Would <u>ja do</u> faster work, in picking the <u>plums</u>?

180. to help: **won-go-ha-da** (v.)

After he <u>won, Joe</u> had a desire to <u>help</u> others.

181. to protect: **bo-ho-ha-da** (v.)

- <u>Bo, ho! Hada</u> has no need for you to <u>protect</u> her! She's as tough as they come, a real bruiser.

182. to support: **ji-ji-ha-da**

Imagine: <u>Chi-Chi</u> (close to <u>ji-ji</u>) the <u>Chi</u>huahua needs <u>support</u>, due to "Little Man Syndrome."

183. to preserve, conserve: **bo-jon-ha-da**

- <u>Bo, Joan had a</u> wish to <u>preserve</u>/Things few others would want to <u>conserve</u>!

184. statistic (info): **tong-gye**

- What are the <u>stats</u> on <u>dogs</u> (gye → gae) that get sick from bad <u>cans</u> (<u>tong</u>) of dog food?

185. be rotten: **bu-pae-ha-da** (v.) (adj. = bu-pae-han)

- At this <u>buffet</u> (close to <u>bu-pae</u>), all the food items are <u>rotten</u>.

186. rumor, hearsay: **so-mun** (n.)
- "<u>So, Moon</u>ies were involved in some shady practices? That's just a <u>rumor</u>, I think." (Disclaimer: no allegations here, this is just a mnemonic device.)

187. respect (honor): **jon-jung-ha-da** (v.)
- "In China, many sci-fi fans <u>honor</u> James Earl <u>Jon</u>es (jon), as Darth Vader's™ voice. (n. = jon-jung)"

188. respect (admire): **jon-gyeong-ha-da**
- Imagine that <u>geeky young</u> (<u>gyeong</u>) fanboys (and older ones, too) <u>admire</u> James Earl <u>Jones</u> as Darth Vader's™ voice.

189. responsibility, duty: **chae-gim** (spelled "chaek-im")
- We have a <u>duty</u> to <u>check 'im</u> out, to make sure he's not a bad guy.

190. to command, order: **myeong-nyeong-ha-da** (v.)
- <u>MYEONG</u>! <u>NYEONG</u>! (loud chewing sounds)
- I <u>command</u> you to eat your food more quietly!

191. to be comfortable: **pyeon-ha-da** (v.) (adj. = pyeon-han)
- "In chess, if you have a good <u>pawn</u> (close to pyeon) structure, you'll often have a <u>comfortable</u> middle game."

192. composer (musical): **jak-gok-ga**
- "<u>Jack, Coker go</u>t a lot of caffeine. Not good for a <u>musical composer</u>.

193. concentrate: **jip-jung-ha-da** (v.)
- Get your <u>jeep, Joong,</u> and head out to the sticks. You can't <u>concentrate</u> in the noisy downtown area. (n. = jip-jung)

194. hat, or sports cap: **mo-ja** (n.)
- <u>Moe</u>, <u>car</u> (ja → <u>cha</u>, "car") brand <u>hats</u> are not my favorite <u>hats</u>.

195. to transport: **su-song-ha-da**
Imagine an Air France plane is <u>transport</u>ing <u>Sue</u>. She hears the "<u>son</u>" (French for "sound" → SOHNG) of French music on her earphones.

196. to be energetic, vigorous: **ssik-ssik-ha-da** (v.)
Imagine a pair of <u>sheiks</u> (<u>ssik</u>) who are very <u>energetic</u>.

197. bicycle: **ja-jeon-geo** (n.)
- Someone in a <u>car</u> (ja)* pulls up next to <u>Chun</u>-li (<u>jeon</u>, "Street Fighter®" character), who is on her <u>bicycle</u>. They stutter, "<u>Cuh-Cuh</u>-Can you t-t-tell me...?" (<u>geo</u>)
* (ja → cha)

198. to be grouchy: **si-mu-ruk-ha-da** (v.)
- <u>Shimu, rooks</u> (close to "ruk") in Western chess can make one <u>grouchy</u>, because they get trapped easily.

199. lighthouse: **deung-dae** (n.)
- <u>During</u> (<u>deung</u>, said quickly) <u>dae</u> (day), <u>lighthouses</u> aren't really needed.

200. student: **hak-saeng** (n.)
- "The <u>student</u> listened, as the <u>crane bird</u> (<u>hak</u>) <u>sang</u> (saeng)." (Quite cacophonic!)

201. to need, require: **pi-ryo-ha-da** (v.)
- <u>Rain</u> (bi → pi) was <u>needed</u> in <u>Rio</u> (ryo), after a long dry spell there. (n. = pi-ryo)

202. to compromise: **ta-hyeop-ha-da** (v.)
- "We reached a <u>compromise</u> on our T.V. watching. I watch the <u>music program</u> (Ta-daa!) one week, he watches the <u>horse show</u> (giddy <u>hup</u> → <u>hyeop</u>) the following week. (n. = ta-hyeop)

203. toilet (bowl): **pyeon-gi**

- "You peon (→ pyeon)! Ghee (gi) isn't meant to be flushed down the toilet (even if it's rancid)!

204. to talk, speak: **mal-ha-da**

- "A T.V. horse (mal), Mr. Ed®, could speak! (mal)

205. frequent (adj.): **bin-beon-han**

- "The bean bun, Han, frequently serves as a comfort food for me."

206. tie, draw, stalemate (n.): **mu-seung-bu** Ramu, to get a win (???) against Boo (bu) is very hard; you'd be lucky to get a draw.

207. **jeon-dang-po**: pawn shop, secondhand shop
Imagine that Chun-Li (Street Fighter character) has a small portable stove for "jeon" (Korean pancakes), and also a small soup mixer (change "dang" to "tang" or soup). She goes to a pawn shop to pawn them off. The clerk at the store is "Po" (Kung Fu Panda character).

208. **jeong-jeon**: black out, or power outage
Imagine that Chun-Li (Street Fighter Character) is cooking "jeon" (Korean pancakes) on an electric stove. There is

"Wang Chung" (UK pop band) music playing on a stereo in the background. Suddenly, there is a blackout, and all the power goes off.

Recommended and Inspirational Books:

(1) "Handbook of Korean Vocabulary" by Choo and O'Grady (you <u>must</u> buy this!)

(2) "Teach Yourself Korean" by Vincent and Yeon

(3) "Basic Sentence Patterns in Korean" by John H. Koo

(4) Almost anything by Hollym Books and Tuttle Books (including their dictionaries).

(5) VocabuLearn series for Korean (by Penton Overseas)

(6) "Unforgettable Languages" (for Korean) (unforgettablelanguages.com)

(7) Mastering Korean Vocabulary by Paul DeGennaro (Lulu Books)

(8) "Learn Japanese Verbs and Adjectives Using Memory Mnemonics" by Ryan McDonald (Trafford Publishing)

(9) "The Intermediate Spanish Memory Book" by Harrison & Welker

(10) "Moonwalking With Einstein" by Josh Foer

(11) "The Quick and Dirty Guide to Learning Languages Fast" by A.G. Hawke

Printed in the United States
by Baker & Taylor Publisher Services